First Edition

ISBN 978-1-9996363-2-6

Published by Inner Version Ltd
www.innerversion.com

XLI — DUAL IGNITION

I. Sparks are best afforded
        To small portions
        Of new source material.

II. Breathing freshly
        On warm embers
        Ignites spontaneously.

XLII — SLOW VIRTUES

I. The future honours
   The past for perseverance.

II. Pondering ambiguity
   Surprises with later fulfilment.

III. The long relationship
   Appreciates in need the time invested.

IV. Living sustainably
   Acts from the deeper self.

XLIII — FIRST CREATION

I.   The initial burst
         Contains the magic of creation.

II. Meditation preserves
         The fresh perspective.

III. Absent time
         Returns toward the start.

I.   Appreciation of the moment
        Builds for the duration
           Of the spell.

II.   Untainted circles of experience
        Naturally can overlap
        Without explanation.

III.   The art requires
        Nothing external
For the magic to continue.

XLV — FULLER CONTEXT

I.   Initial context
        Is lost in headlines magnified.

II.   Early judgement
        Requires extra effort to overrule.

III.   Impartially viewing
        The fuller picture
        Preserves intended meaning.

IV.   Completely quoting
        Information gives deceit
        No chance to grow.

I.   Further growth
        Upon a branch
        Of assumed knowledge
    Keeps the branch alive.

II.   Pruning near the base
        Of a great branch
            Grown crooked and untrue
    Requires strength,
    Accepts that dazzling flowers
        Reappear on true growth.

XLVII — UNFINISHED EXPLORATION

I.   Not all routes
        Require initial exploration.

II.   Fullness can be found
        In the unique set
        Of paths crossed.

III.   The rhythm of the unexplored
        Resonates the future self
           In fantastic ways.

I.   Mundane information
      Adds weight
      To links in the chain;
Fascinating knowledge
      Lightens the chain,
      Eases oscillation.

II.   Dullness of delivery
      Thickens friction, waves halt nearby;
Playful communication
      Lowers friction,
      Waves propagate
      Far and wide.

I. Aggregations of deeper knowledge
   Require more effort
    To gain momentum.

II. Early supporters
   With profound intuitive sense
  Know where to apply
   Their precious force.

III. Shallow thought
   Maintains inertia;
  Thought deepens,
   Inertia rises.

L — THOUGHT TRAVERSAL

I.   Depth-first work
        Hunts down the target
            With minimal effort;
    Breadth-first work
    Gathers resources
        To plan ahead.

II.   Depth-first knowledge
        Adds quirk and fascination;
    Breadth-first knowledge
    Balances the character.

III. Depth-first exploration
        Delves into the inner version
            To reveal higher connections;
    Breadth-first exploration
    Understands the current space
        To prepare for deeper levels.

I. The number of domains
   To be mastered
Is limited only
   By time accessible.

II. Multiple fields of thought
Prevents extraneous obsession.

III. The repeated shift
   Between multiplicity
And unity in thought
   Reveals all opportunities.

I.   Experience is received
         From a remote time and place
         Of a problem almost identical.

II. Adapting the solution before
         Contains a path
         Of minimal effort.

III. Precious time is diverted
         Shortly after the answer
         Is confirmed.

LIII — MOVING AVERAGE

I. Setbacks toward the start
    Seemingly provoke
        The short-term moving average.

II. Sources of lasting joy
    Amplify unseen
        The long-term moving average.

I.   Acknowledging pieces to improve
        In the inherited parcel
        Is a magnificent step.

II.   Adding jewels unearthed
        Each day, the parcel
        Gifted to the future
            Is made more valuable.

I.   Routine reinforces
        Positive structure;
    New routes expand
        Beyond previous constraints.

II.   Non-motion settles
        Patterns of thought;
    Exercise initiates
        Winds of change.

III.   The selective diary
        Of positive thought
    Elevates alternate pathways
        From the source unlimited.

LVI — SELF IMAGINED

I.   Failure vividly imagined
        Succeeds in reproducing failure;
Success spurred on
        By will alone
        Fails to enforce success.

II.   In the presence
        Of two opposing forces,
        Imagination takes precedence
Over power of will.

III.   The positive self-affirmation —
        Repeated twenty times at night
Eventually invokes
        The power of the imagination.

IV.   Every day,
And in every respect,
I am getting better and better.

I.   Arrogance insists
        On extreme self-importance;
    Confidence emanates
        From masterful self-control.

II.   Selflessness shifts the soul
        Beyond the usual limits;
    Self-sacrifice does not require
        Crossing the harmful boundary.

I.   Only a minute subset
        Of total skill is called
        Upon in daily action.

II.   Identical training for work
        Nevertheless allows the infinite
        Array of new interpretations.

III.   Small pieces of specialised
        Knowledge occasionally produce
        Results of sparkling beauty.

LIX — TOTAL IMAGE

I. The individual appears
        As a singular fraction
        Of the total image.

II. The limitations of role and species
        Achieve fullness
        In the larger group.

III. Generations of anonymous
        Entities progress;
    The sustaining form
        Remains in timelessness.

IV. Social participation
        Realises the all in the individual;
    Meditation in exile
        Reveals the self in all.

I.   High influence
         Tends to omit the required proof;
     Low influence
         Tends to misplace the needed effort.

II. Corruption multiplies
         With oligarchy, isolated leaders;
     Thought narrows
         With monarchy, solitary leader;
     The world opens
         With anarchy, equal influence.

I.   The burdened masses
      Of thought
         Orbit a common centre
      Of over-attachment.

II.   The traveller practises
      Leaving self-restricting circles
         By releasing attachment
      To the world of forms,
Returning dutifully
      To reinitiate the self.

LXII — WITHIN REDEMPTION

I.   No amount
        Of unwise judgement
    Passes beyond redemption.

II.   The smaller scale
        Is closely examined,
    Inter-being boundaries
        Relinquish definition.

III.   The larger universe
        Is deeply realised,
    Required forgiveness
        Flows within.

LXIII — SKILFUL UNDERSTANDING

I.   The patient listener
Studies suffering
     To develop compassion,
Inquires deeply
     To develop understanding.

II.   The skilful teacher
Adapts the truth
     Without inconsistency,
Uses peaceful language
     Without exaggeration.

I.   The delicate proposal
     Precisely gathers
          Current knowledge,
     Implicitly credits
          Earlier wisdom.

II. The new way of being
     Clearly promotes
          Without opposing,
     Fairly disrupts
          Without contention.

I.   All dreams have potential
        To influence behaviour
    And thus are woven
        Into universal history.

II.   The isolated system
        Imagines self-harm
        Without effect on others.

III.   The simple law
        Harms no being unessentially.

IV.   My body returns
        To the universe
    When my good work is done.

LXVI — NATURAL BEING

I. Connected presence
   Rediscovers the force sustaining.

II. Accordance with nature
    Resonates the great wheel.

I. The legacy of the past
    Is subject entirely to needs
    And opinions of the future.

II. The self
    Observes itself
    From many points of view.

III. The living universe
    Has a legacy only
    As the whole being.

I.   There is no edge
          To infinite space
          Or space repeating.

II.   In a universe where
          Every point is central,
     Self-realisation can occur
          In any place.

III.   Each undiscovered scene
          In time and space
     Contains an opportunity
          As yet unseen
     To be centred in the self.

I. Learning aims
    For pleasure,
    Not for relative advantage.

II. The gift of knowledge
    Disperses into the world
    Without dilution.

III. Aiming nowhere
    Lives in harmony,
    Listens to reality.

I.   The humble surface
         Holds in reserve knowledge
         Of the power immeasurable.

II. The universal deep
         Contains such undiscovered treasures
         Of joy beyond imagination.

I. Distant patterns
   Etched into residual memory
Allow unique interpretations.

II. Clear visions
   To earlier conditions
Occasionally appear.

III. Improvisations built respectfully
   Around the original image
Inherit equal fascination.

I.   The fruits of labour past
        Offer fierce temptation
        To be closely guarded.

II.   Each spontaneous moment
        Contains experience unique
        To the point in time.

III.   The divine right to create
        Has inspiration received
From the one source
        Masquerading as the many.

I. Not all senses operate
    At equal frequency.

II. Prolonged perception
    Enhances the moment.

III. Slow digestion
    Extracts the highest nutrients.

I.   The virtual indicator
       Of the speed of thought
   Becomes clearer
       With meditation practice.

II.   Quality of energy
       Transforms at high speed;
   The underlying universe
       Appears at zero speed.

III.   Returning focus
       To the dial
   Improves direct control
       Of the thought process.

IV.   The force held high
       Advances culture;
   The force held low
       Deepens awareness.

LXXV — BEYOND DESCRIPTION

I.   Created worlds
      Of forms contrasting
      Can be easily described.

II.   The singular existence
      Has no lack or surplus,
      Has no other point of reference.

III.   The highest spirits
   Represent the step penultimate
      Before eternity.

IV.   The uncreated world
      Beyond description
   Can be experienced
      Through meditation.

LXXVI — PAIRS UNIFIED

I. Pain and pleasure,
Birth and death —
Are one
    In the presence of everything.

II. Eternity and time,
The world and nothingness —
Are the same
    When everything is in the present.

LXXVII — COSMIC DEPENDENCE

I.   The destiny of the cosmic
            Is intertwined with
     The fate of the microscopic.

II.   The universe is not a set
          Of separate
          Independent
          Objects —
     Precise dividing boundaries
          Between labelled items of cognition
     Cannot be defined.

III.   Continuous dependence
          On all scales of change
     Is the natural process
          Of the cosmos.

I. The present situation
        Creatively rephrased
        Assures the self.

II. Truly scalable ambition
        Is relative entirely
        To the individual.

III. The zeniths of achievement
        Owe at least in part
        To favourable conditions.

IV. Setting out and rising
        To new substantial heights
        Counts as complete success.

LXXIX — THE INCOMPLETE

I.   The new piece
        Of knowledge moves
    No closer to completion.

II.   The illusion
        Of the finite clings
    To variations viewed complete.

III.   Where no entire knowledge
        Of the field can be acquired,
            Interest arises.

IV.   To be a work in progress
        Is to realise
            The infinity of the incomplete.